I ONCE WAS BLIND

VOL 1

KEITH AND TIERA BRYANT

I Once Was Blind…

ISBN: 978-1-7337342-4-0 (Paperback)

First printing, 2020

The Bryants
P.O. Box 7053
Columbus, GA 31908
Ioncewasblind2@gmail.com
www.ioncewasblind.com

Tiera Bryant

To my wife,
I'm so proud of the woman you have become. Sticking with you
through it all, was worth it. You are my "sweet suga". ~ Keith

Dedication Page

"Thanks be unto God which always causes us to triumph"!
2 Corinthians 2:14 (KJV)

I dedicate this book to my firstborn child, Kei'Orah Bryant. I apologize for every burden that I placed on you during my broken season. You are one of the reasons for me to shift and become the woman that I am blossoming into. Thanks to my parents for birthing me and giving me all that you guys had and have. I love you all. Thanks to my husband for walking with me on this journey. To my other two kids Hannah and Elijah Bryant I promise to make you guys proud as your mother. ~ Tiera

FOREWORD

Every once in a while, you meet people whose life story is only rivaled by what you've seen in a movie or read in a book. Keith and Tiera Bryant totally fit that description. From small humble beginnings to successful community leaders and business owners, their story offers hope on many levels. I have had the pleasure of watching them grow, as individuals and as a couple. I have served as a spiritual leader and covering for them for a number of years now and this book is only a small portion of what's to come that will change the lives of many.

Using the phrase "sight beyond what I see" helps with laying the foundation for what they are releasing to you in this book. To say that all have eyes, and still cannot see, gives definition to the condition today know as blindness. As a couple, they reveal what a "normal" life for many who grow up in rural America look like. It is not a slap in the face or a belittling, just a glimpse into what growing up without hope and vision – and the impact of their absence.

It takes great courage and confidence to share personal stories and struggles that do not reveal the most pleasant days of your life. Yet, it is a calling that must be answered if we are ever going to reach out to others in an attempt to challenge cultural barriers and norms that are present in our communities. I want to guarantee you that having insight into their journey will add value to your life and help you to answer the call for yourself.

Jesus did not come to those who were well, He came to those who needed a doctor and healing. Like Jesus, this book is being sent into the Earth with a similar mission and mandate. It is not meant to be read from a religious backdrop, it is being released as a tool to bring light to those who are sitting in darkness. Never before have we needed more transparency and authenticity than we do now. It is my prayer that this book inspires you to start the dialogue concerning vision and progress; that it challenges you to never settle for anything less than God's vision for your life.

It is with great joy that I join in with them on their assignment! May your eyes be opened, your hope be restored, and your faith be increased... like the blind man in the Bible – may you too say that "I once was blind, but now I see".

APOSTLE CHRISTIAN T. HOWELL SR.
- OVERCOMERS MOVEMENT
Board Certified Advanced Life Coach & Biblical Cognitive Behavioral Therapist
Author of *"Chosen & Challenged"*, *"I Feel You... Walking Out of Domestic Violence"*, and other books

THE JOURNEY BEGINS

It can be quite challenging to have a clear and great vision for your life when you grow up in a small town. Your world often appears cloudy and the people that you are surrounded by are likely just existing. They are physically moving, as far as working and day-to-day activities, but there is no real movement or progress. You realize that the issue with them, and yourself is visual blindness. We had no vision. If we did, it rarely exceeded where or how we were currently living. We were rich in time but concerning vision we were in poverty.

Poverty can be defined as the state of a person or family who lacks a socially acceptable amount of money or material possessions for what they need, not want. Poverty exists in every city and in every culture. It always has, and I believe that it always will to some extent. Poverty has an uncomfortable and unmistakable feel to it. The atmosphere of poverty is like a dark black hole spinning around in a circle. I should know… I grew up in it.

As I recall it, everyone was doing the same thing. They were all driving the same cars, working jobs they barely enjoyed or were satisfied with, living for the weekends, and trying to outdo the next person. People were selling drugs or had a hustle on every corner. Very few of us really prospered out of low-income communities. Don't get me wrong, I am not ashamed of how I grew up. It is what helped motivate and propel me to my NOW!

In our country, most low-income living areas are perverted and controlled by poverty mindsets. I would estimate that 50 to 80 percent of the people who do have a decent paying job have to commute at least 45 minutes to work one way. There aren't enough resources there to support the people. Most of the people in the area are working from paycheck to paycheck. The most exciting part of the week was consumed with "living for the weekend". It was the "best part of life". As a matter of fact, I used to live for the weekend which usually consisted of "club hopping". I had never considered saving money, leaving a legacy, or writing a will; neither did any of my peers.

As a little girl, I used to dream of having a huge house, lots of money, and owning my own businesses. As a child, you just dream as you're playing with your doll houses, kitchen sets, and houseware toys. I would imagine I was living a life full of purpose and satisfaction. Although I didn't understand the meaning of purpose at that very moment, I would always dream of having a bright future, even though I grew up in a "bootleg" house. Let me explain why I say that. In that environment, I saw things that I should not have been exposed to at my age. By the age of 9, I could name every beer, liquor, and cigarette that was on the shelves of the stores. Cursing and arguing were the norm. As I grew up, I thought that was the proper way to communicate with those I liked or loved.

Kids will usually adapt to what they see, not what they are told. I developed a language full of vulgar curse words. I would yell obscenities at babies, kids, and adults alike. All of this was seed for my healthy dream and vision to grow dim and obscure at best. At least I had one safe and happy place. At home, inside my room with my doll house, I felt as if I mattered and had purpose. When I left my room, the negativity and the darkness overwhelmed my purpose.

Growing up, I didn't travel with my parents or take family trips. No disrespect to my parents, they provided and gave me the best life they could with the resources that they had at the time. For my vacation, I would tell my dolls we were going on a vacation to wherever I dreamed of going. When my make-believe vacation was over, I would tell myself that I would leave my hometown as soon as I graduated from high school. As I grew older and became a teenager, my vision and dreams quickly faded away. Those seeds of distortion from my childhood began to take root and the weeds quickly grew. I remember putting my dolls down and starting to look at my surroundings more intently. I looked and I watched... I looked and I watched...

All the negativity fought for and grabbed my attention...

Year after year, month after month, day after day, and little by little I became more aware of my current reality of poverty. Eventually, I allowed it to grab my vision and ultimately choke it out until it just faded away. The picture that I once had for my life when I was a child was lost as an adult. I could not see it for myself no matter how hard I tried. I had been suddenly blinded, and I didn't immediately realize it or try to find a cure for it!!!!

Here I was in high school with no vision, yet I used to dream of starting and finishing college. My vision was so distorted. I didn't even know what to go to college for. I had no clue what degree to pursue or what career I wanted. In hindsight, everyone else had ideas and plans for my future except me. I allowed my surroundings and upbringing to shape and mold me.

At that time, all I knew was shopping and living for the moment, riding around hitting the same three blocks. I started attending college just to get a school check, not to learn or finish it. I learned that behavior by listening and watching other people do that same thing. I was consumed with poverty and didn't even know it. As a matter of fact, I was dating a good young man who made sure my needs and wants were met. Even still, I was building a pile of personal debt. I brought my own shovel and dug a hole for myself that would take a long time to come out of.

One of the worst parts of this story is that so many people wrote me off. All they saw was this young girl with this drug dealer. I was counted as a loss by so many people that were close to me. At the same time, many of those same folks did their best to control or destroy our relationship with their words and thoughts. Because they saw no good, they did not do or say anything to help us. I guess since they saw no vision of our future, they treated us as if we had little value.

This is what I constantly heard from others - words like "You are not going to make it", "You'll never be anything more than a high school dropout", or "He's going to destroy you and anything that you ever try to do". These are the words that caused me so much doubt and unbelief in myself.

These were word curses and thoughts that tried to manifest and had to be fought and broken before I could ever see myself being happy and prospering.

Most people thought that my man had something to do with my stagnation. However, if it was up to him, I would be a millionaire by NOW! He would always encourage me to go to college or to start my own business. "Go and make something out of yourself," he would constantly tell me. This man saw the best in me. He was always in the background cheering me on. For the life of him, he couldn't understand why I wouldn't go and be successful. He was literally giving me the world. There was nothing I had need of. The problem was I was blinded.

The first time he ever spoke to me he said, "I want to give you the world and help you leave here". Unfortunately, by the time we met, and I let him into my life, my vision was already gone. I had become blind. I heard the words that he spoke, but I couldn't see them for myself. My mind was extremely cloudy. My mind was not connected to any purpose for myself. By this time in my life, I was asking "What purpose?" ... "What is my purpose?".

After giving birth to my first child at the age of 19, he really tried to push me to build a legacy. He wanted something legit, something legal, and something that was stable. He understood that the lifestyle we were living included no guarantees or security. It wasn't something that you could do for a lifetime without real and lasting consequences and we were parents now.

Life outside my house... I'm glad that you asked.

I spent most of my childhood at my grandmother's house every day. I only went home to get clothes or other small items. It was nothing to see people get drunk and smoke all day long, from sunup to sundown. I watched people spend their entire paycheck on one day: Friday. Sometimes they would use credit all week long and they would pay my grandmother on Friday when they got off work. I watched the older people meet up and cheat on each other right in my grandmother's house.

My grandmother lived in a double wide trailer. The kitchen and living room were open with nothing separating the two. The stove was right by the back door. One night I was standing in the kitchen cooking a beef patty. It was a full house as normal. A man opened the back door and commanded his girlfriend to come out. She was hugged up in the living room with another man. She didn't respond nor did she move. There I was still prancing around at the stove around the age of 10. The guy pulled a gun out and shot in the living room. The bullet went right past the side of my face. If I would've moved, I would've been shot. Instead, it went out through the living room window. My grandmother tussled with him and took the gun and beat him up. My grandmother was like "Madea" LOL! Literally!!

If there's nothing else I know for sure it's that the devil comes to kill, steal, and destroy.

At that moment, the enemy crept in and I became afraid. I was traumatized. As I recall it, no one ever asked me how I felt or even asked me if I was okay. After that night, I began to have uncontrollable thoughts of dying. As if that wasn't bad enough, the thoughts got worse. Then the enemy began torturing me with the fear of dying. Fear took over me as a little girl. I would be brushing my teeth, then I would have thoughts like, "You are going to die… you have to die". I would just start crying and screaming. For years and years, the enemy tormented me with that thought...

Fast forward…I only saw myself working entry-level retail jobs. I'm not saying that anything is wrong with working those jobs, because they serve and fulfill a purpose like every other job. The problem was that I lived and worked only to see my food stamps. I trusted in the government more than God. I saw how my peers would lose their minds on food stamp day. Guess what??? I did too!! To be honest, the food stamps given to me wouldn't even last the whole month. LOL! I had no sense of budget or spending responsibly. Yeah, I know this is real talk...

Writing a business plan and thinking of legitimate ways to make real money was the last thing on my mind. I couldn't see myself as a business owner, I was just trying to keep a job, not even trying to make more than minimum wage.

There was a man who was pulling me by the hand, telling me to "Come on"… "You are somebody" … "You are better than what you see".

I looked and saw my daughter, but I was consumed by blindness and my feet wouldn't move. My heart wanted more, but I felt powerless to do anything about it. The devil lied to me and said that I wasn't worthy. So here we are playing tug-a-war on the inside, while to the world I was looking as if I had it made. Many wanted to be in my shoes, or so they thought. I would say to myself that I couldn't see my way out. I was blind... I was confused... My dreams were pushed so far in the back of my mind, and the distortions, distractions, and disappointments washed out my vision.

Even with all that you've heard so far, there was something on the inside of me that wasn't ever satisfied. My heart would cry out on the inside when I would hear my daughter's voice. We were trying to give her everything we didn't get from our parents growing up. We were trying hard, but my heart still wasn't satisfied.

As an adult parent, my days consisted of walking up and down the road, going from house to house gossiping about whatever was going on and about each other. If the police, firetruck, or ambulance went anywhere, the whole neighborhood would follow. If a fight broke out, the whole town showed up. Literally, the whole town! We would stand there until the end of the fight. No purpose, no vision, no life. To the shock of many, I was a willing participant in all of this.

Everyone knew which day we got our food stamps. We all would get up early and go grocery shopping on the same day we received our benefits. You had a set day of each month when you'd receive your benefits. The day before I got mine, I would have my day all planned out--- I was ready!! I used to get mine on the 9th of the month. Because I grew up watching people borrowing food stamps and selling them, guess what I did? The same thing.

I thought getting Medicaid and food stamps were the only forms of assistance. I didn't even know anything about the benefits of health, dental, and vision insurance. Having life insurance was totally irrelevant. Everyone would be upset and complain about not having enough money to buy health insurance and to be honest, I felt the same way. However, I didn't want a job that would have me making too much money, because then I'd be over the income bracket of receiving Medicaid and food stamps. Medicaid and food stamps can be beneficial when used properly, but it should not be our vision of how we take care of ourselves. Use it for what it is worth when it's needed. If we would use them properly, we wouldn't be bound to them or bound by them – living a lifestyle that they solely permit. It is a system that is set up by man.

John 15:19 (ESV) tells us, "If you were of the world, the world would love you as its own; but because you are not of the world, but I chose you out of the world, therefore the world hates you".

"My prayer is not that you take them out of the world but that you protect them from the evil one. They are not of the world, even as I am not of it" John 17:15-16 (KJV)

My Relationship

Living with and dating a known drug dealer, I found myself in plenty of life or death situations. I was willingly jeopardizing my life and freedom. No matter how much he would try to keep me away from being in the environment, it just wasn't happening. I was deeply in love and all I wanted was to be there in his presence. He would leave to go get drugs without telling me to keep me from going. Even that would cause an argument. To keep me quiet, he would sometimes take me. I would be scared, but still wanted to go. I knew what the outcome could've been. I wanted to be there. I wanted to go. He never asked me to hold, sell, or go get any drugs for him. I never did any of it, I was just there in the midst of it all. I held down his passenger seat.

There would be times I didn't know if he would make it out of some of the trap houses that we would go to. Everyone knows the dangers of that lifestyle in College Park, GA. If not, it was one of the most dangerous and drug infested areas of Atlanta, GA. We would set-up shop and operate in that area. Everyone in the room had guns. We would meet people at different places in that area. The people we would meet, would send people before they came themselves to scope us out. Even though I was blind, God had a plan and vision for my life...

We had gotten stopped several times by law enforcement of various levels of government. Every time they would stop us, there wouldn't be anything on us. This one time we got stopped, and we had something on us, it was the drug task force who stopped us. I was on the passenger side as usual. The agent immediately hand cuffed him and told me not to move. The agent pulled him like 100 feet from the car. The other officers stood behind the vehicle and watched me. I didn't move a muscle. I just started praying. They asked me to get out of the car. Then they stood us side by side. For some reason, the officer thought I was someone familiar. He ran our information, but nothing came back.

One of the officers searched the vehicle inside out. While the other one waited with us, he kept trying to tell us what would happen if he found drugs. He told us he received a phone call that we were on the way to get drugs. I kept quiet and was praying in my head. I was blind, but I wasn't dumb! The officer didn't find any drugs. Instead, he found the evidence that we used to hide the drugs. Thank God the vehicle was junky with paper, bags, teddy bears, etc. He asked us about a few items, and he kept looking.

"Call upon Me in the day of trouble; I shall rescue you, and you will honor Me."
-Psalm 50:15 (NASB)

The officer that was standing with us was the one in charge. He called the other officer from the vehicle. He uncuffed my boyfriend at the time, my now husband, and he told us to go and have a safe trip back home. He apologized for wasting our time. That was the longest ride EVER to get home. My heart was beating so fast! I couldn't hardly calm down until we made it home.

"For I know the plans I have for you," declares the LORD, "plans to prosper you and not to harm you, plans to give you hope and a future."
Jeremiah 29:11 (NIV)

All this time I knew full well what could happen. Just remember, I had never seen anything other than poverty and I wanted to feel like I belonged. Even though he would show me all the love he could possibly give, I was only comfortable in dysfunction. I still felt like I had to prove my love and loyalty to him, but it wasn't what he wanted or asked me to do.

Even though we didn't deserve it, thank God for His mercy! It is renewed every morning. He loved us so much and that was not the plan nor the vision He had for me nor my husband. That was a trap from hell. God stepped in and said "NO"!! Even though we were totally wrong, I believe with everything in me that God confused the officer and hid the drugs.

"I will send my terror ahead of you and throw into confusion every nation you encounter. I will make all your enemies turn their backs and run."
-Exodus 23:27 (NIV)

"Then the LORD said to me, "You have seen well, for I am [actively] watching over My word to fulfill it."
Jeremiah 1:12 (AMP)

While all of this was going on, there was something on the inside of me that was never satisfied. My heart would still cry on the inside when I would hear my daughter's voice. Although I was currently blind towards my purpose and my future, I now know that my vision wasn't dead, I just had lost sight of it.

One day I was invited to a church service. I agreed to go, and I went religiously because going was the "right thing to do" and "that's where you go when you have problems". You see, I used to pray as a child and read the children's Bible so I always knew deep inside that there was a chance that it could help. As you can see, I always knew to pray. I went thinking it was going to be a regular and typical Sunday service. One of the leaders of the church began to pray and worship got more and more intense. The mother of the church looked at me and gave me one word, she said "Breakthrough". She pointed at me and kept repeating "Breakthrough".

I didn't know what was going on, but God started doing something on the inside of me. It was my first time ever feeling God's presence. Those of you who have ever felt His presence know what I mean. I had to go back the next week to see if this was real. No one in there was physically touching me and my tears just flowed uncontrollably. God heard my heart's cry and was answering it!

God's word touched me in a way that I cannot really explain. He washed me with His blood. His presence overwhelmed me. His love filled my heart. As I sat there in the church, I cried hysterically telling God "YES"! I remember it all as if it was just yesterday!

The preacher expounded on how we need Jesus as our personal savior and why He died for us. The preacher explained why we were created. Afterwards, the preacher did an altar call for anyone who had never accepted Jesus as their Lord and savior. I went up to accept Jesus as my Lord and savior. I cried out on the floor and the leaders of the church embraced and surrounded me with love. It was an answer to a longing in my heart – a healthy family.

The ministers explained to me the importance of reading my Bible. They laid hands on me and prayed. Afterwards, I got in my Bible like never before. I began to read and study- my hunger was real. I went to every bible study for at least four months straight and for me that was an unusual level of commitment. I began to learn about who God is and the many people that God worked through.

I thank God for guiding me to that church. I used to call my daughter bad. That's what my parents and all the adults in my family called us. I was repeating the same cycle. One day the Elder of the church heard me call Kei'Orah "bad". She told me, "Life and death are in the power of your tongue. Your baby will be what you call her". She spoke with such great love and compassion. She asked me, "How does she act every time you call her bad?" I froze. I thought about how every time I called her "bad", she got worse. She told me to start calling her "sweet" and to speak positive words full of life to her.

"Death and life are in the power of the tongue, and those who love it will eat its fruits." Proverbs 8:21 (ESV)

Becoming a mother at a young age was mentally challenging. I can now admit that I didn't know how to properly raise a child. I grew up with being dropped off at my grandmother's house every day. Most of the time I went home just to get clothes. I did the same thing and I can speak for most women in my bloodline and community because they did it also. Some are still exhibiting the same behavior to this day.

That is what we saw and that is what happened to us! My grandmother raised us. The only child-rearing knowledge we possessed was to buy the child material things, scream, fuss, and holler. We never had anyone to ask us how we felt or what choice did we want. If we voiced our opinions, we got cursed and yelled at.

Not only did God renew my mind, He gave me a new language. I learned how to speak His language. When I say that God changes you, I mean He changes all of you! My language began to change from poverty, death, and defeat to success, life, and victory. When I finally connected to God properly, I was able to healthily see God's original purpose and plan for my life. This journey has led to the beginning of many new things and a whole new world of opportunities for me. I can now excitedly declare that I am standing in the door of new things that I never knew were meant for me.

God created us in the likeness of His image. It is the will of our heavenly Father for us to live a healthy life. If I could share any wisdom with you, I would tell you to listen to your kids and allow them to have a voice. Uplift your kids and speak life to them and over them. Never kill their dream or vision but take time to help them define it and to set goals towards them. Create a healthy and consistent routine for your life and with God as the Leader, you will avoid the trap of diminished vision and blindness. Jesus came to give us life and that more abundantly. He gives us the power to get wealth.

"But thou shalt remember the Lord thy God: for it is he that giveth thee power to get wealth, that he may establish his covenant which he sware unto thy fathers, as it is this day" (Deuteronomy 8:18, KJV).

I cannot tell it all right now, but I will share a quick summary of all the magnificent blessings that I received, once my vision started clearing up.

Since I surrendered my heart to Christ, I obtained a decent paying job with the court system. For the first time in my adult life, I was earning more than minimum wage. I wasn't even qualified for this job. I did not have any experience regarding the job requirements. I decreed and declared every day that I would have a job. All I can say is that once you shift your focus and work your faith, the heavens will unlock. I was walking under an open heaven.

At this time, I was quite extravagant with my outward appearance. I could be seen wearing purple hair and purple nails. I removed the purple hair pieces and changed the color on my nails. I told my nail tech that I had an interview and I needed to look professional. She asked me where my interview was and I told her that I didn't know yet, but someone was going to call me. I purchased an outfit for this nonexistent interview, and I hung it in my closet. Every day I would decree out of my mouth that someone is going to call me for an interview.

During this time, I didn't allow my phone battery to go dead and every time my phone would ring, I answered it. I did this for 3 months because I was in expectation. Within those 3 months I filled out numerous job applications. No one would call me. I kept getting turned down through emails, but I didn't let that stop me. I understood that faith without works is dead. (James 2:7 KJV). I kept the faith even though the enemy tried to speak otherwise and show me differently. I saw what God spoke and I stood on that alone.

At the end of the 3rd month, I was approached by my school advisor who asked me if I wanted a job. I told her "Yes". I received a called that same day for an interview. I got the job and had not even filled out an application yet. When I filled out the application, I was filling out the W4 and the direct deposit form at the same time.

During all of this, I was in college getting my Associate Degree in Business Management. By this time, I was a wife and mother of 3 biological children. I obtained this job BEFORE graduating college. I was on payroll and my supervisor signed off on my internship hours. I graduated from college with a 3.9 GPA and I was able to do this by the strength of God. The same strength was available 10 years ago, but I was blinded. Blinded by poverty, pain, hurt, and sorrow.

Since then, God graced me to leave that 9 to 5 job. The plan wasn't to stay there. It was only supposed to be temporary. I left that job without even having another job. God took me on a journey and I'm now a business owner. I own and operate 3 online businesses. Prosperity Tax Service, Prosperity Fashion, & Prosperity Intimacy. I was called to be an Entrepreneur. God gave me these 3 and there are several others that I am currently strategizing to launch.

In the community, I'm the founder and leader of the group named "Young & Saved". This group was birthed through prayer & fasting. I lead young adults to Jesus Christ and to become Kingdom Citizens. God had spoken to me years ago that I was called to evangelize. It manifested as "Young & Saved". It is an outreach ministry that reaches young ladies who are currently living a life that God has brought me out of. I value the opportunity that God allows these young ladies to glean from my past experiences as well as my current journey. We are a source of sisterhood and encouragement. I encourage them to fix each other's crown when they are tilted and show them through scripture and practical teaching why Jesus is ALWAYS the answer.

I was prophesied that I would become an author and write several books. I didn't understand what this person was speaking to me then, but I understand it all now. At the time I received this prophecy, being an author was the furthest thing in my view. I was just trying to survive daily. I was at a low point in my life, and I was in search of God. I knew that there was a deeper level to Him, and I wanted to experience that. It's amazing how God uses His chosen vessels to share His truth with you at the most seemingly random times. That prophetic word that I received all those years ago, was unfolding right before my eyes. I give God all the glory. Like the blind man in the Bible, I once was blind, and had no vision, but by His wonderous love and unmerited favor I CAN NOW SEE! I had to see it (in the spirit), before I could see it (in the natural).

www.ingramcontent.com/pod-product-compliance
Lightning Source LLC
Chambersburg PA
CBHW060709280326
41933CB00012B/2358